Sacred Rain

Sacred Rain

GHULAM-SARWAR YOUSOF

PARTRIDGE
A Penguin Random House Company

To order additional copies of this book, contact
Toll Free 800 101 2657 (Singapore)
Toll Free 1 800 81 7340 (Malaysia)
orders.singapore@partridgepublishing.com

www.partridgepublishing.com/singapore

Contents

Reflection at Dawn

Rain . . . all my senses
apprehend the fiery
excitement of ageless trees
restive with the weight of green
sunrises on quivering leaves
the glistening flow
of silken water.

Though whispering
in voices seemingly
alien, i know for a certainty
they are conscious
as in the very core of my being
i too am deeply
sentient of unending
connections, unspeakable
fellowships.

Hangzhou Image

Sipping green tea, misty
at a shady Hangzhou cove

on the moon bridge
across a still reticent
stream of the lake a slender
figure glides by, silent
umbrella sheltering, her
reversed double, striking
yellow in a watery mirror.

Is it the flimsy
shade of a mysterious
maiden, i wonder, blushing
angel, or golden deity?

Rising Sun

The rising sun
brings hope of another day
from behind mountains
across horizons
beyond time itself

but the unrelenting darkness
remains in recesses
of the heart
beyond the sun's reach,
unending hunger

for another light
invisible, overwhelming
infinitely softer
than the floating sun, lighter
than light itself.

Destiny

From night's bed of soft blackness
a triumphant sun emerges
red on waves of living fire

though the assurance of what may be
remains uncertain this is clearly
not just another day
but one ripe with untold potentiality

the intimidating colours, fascinating,
are not customary shades of dawn
matching the feathery
breath of early whispering breezes
or voices of lilting birds

in every relentless second of the sun's
journeying from fire to fire there is
an ominous balance between brilliancy
and destruction
that may yet change destiny.

Exhilaration

as i walked in the garden
perfumed with the scent
of red rose
i heard the call
of the nightingale
and my heart,
it was burnt to ashes.

The Night and I

In the vortex of the deep, softly
breathing night I see
my self awaken yet again, impulsively

seeking out my dream. I wonder
where into ever-reaching expanses
of colourless silence it has gone.

The expectant night looks curiously
at me, starless, watching, waiting.
Entering my realm it encloses me.

A supple mantle of mystery
veils the heart immeasurable
of my interior being.

The night and I fuse into one,
companions in loneliness, inseparable,
in timeless embrace meeting.

Strangers

We hardly speak to each other anymore
a nod here, a sign there, silence
has eaten away at the heart's melody
recollections clouded with melancholy.

The perfectly configured ceremonies
of slavery, time-honoured nuptials
that seemingly made existence momentous
exciting, fresh as doves
pursuing each youthful instant to wring
every drop of essential life from it;
those rituals have waxed empty.

We thought love was all, unimaginable
in its passionate intensity.
But long before we knew in the very
core of our being rosy freshness
had turned musty, destiny, ever uncertain
tainted body and spirit, fields not of harmony,
but theatres of acrimony.

Strangers as ever before
we hardly speak to each other any more,
all that remain are desolate
moments inarticulate, dreams desperate
in unending expanses of memory
tainted by the single *bhava* of bitterness.

Lingering Sadness

Sadness lingers heavy
in the empty recesses
of existence
like a obstinate memory
unwilling to leave
or some ancient stain
upon the expectant soul
that harks to the moment
when joyfully
it will yield to persistent
calls of eternity.

Manifestations

I am the word that sings
in Adam's holy
breath, the turbulent ocean flowing
from every lover's moist eye.

I am the diamond by
the glorious hand of the mighty
sculptor chiseled;
the wind that seemingly

blows in every aimless
direction; the flame that blushes
in the ardent centre
of the mysterious rose.

These am I and more
in countless particles circling
in ceaseless
manifestations returning.

Tiresias Waiting

In my mind's eye I see anxious souls
young and old as endlessly
they come and go, halting momentarily
each unprotesting day in vast
expanses of undifferentiated time.

I wonder whence they come, where
they are heading, if they have any
notion of direction or destination
or if it is their destiny
to merely move forever aimlessly.

Ages have come, ages have gone,
the lingering hills, touching the very
skies, have grown ancient, watching;
the whispering rivers reborn
countless times in constraining streams.

And wrapped in cosmic dreams, I still wait
to move on until the call comes, finally.

Midnight December 31 2011

This precious moment sits precarious
between one day's shadow and the radiance
of another, as one more impatient year
assumes the mantle of its precursor.

The profusely lit-up skies, the unstinting
clamour of midnight voices,
the unbridled revelry provide
more than essential testimony.

Will this be yet another recalling of fading
memories, restoring of persistent anxieties,
well-intentioned resolutions
framed in considered thoughtlessness?

Will this be a repeat season of assurances
or a further spin of drunken celebrations?
Occasion for insightful renewal or merely fifty-
two further weeks in unstinting cycles of futility?

Dawn

The emerging sun dispenses
its precious radiance
through the thin mist of existence.

The silence whispers, its voice
as yet without resonance.

It is the birth of another day
another year another lifetime,
glorious manifestation.

It is yet another conscious
drop, quintessence of eternity.

The Rains are Falling

The rains are falling wildly from afar
not gentle but insistent
as though long repressed, as though
high above, beyond conceivable distances,
has burst the mighty dam that held
the sky's oceans at bay.

Day after each exhausted day
they descend as though our fortunes
in countless stars have never ceased weeping
for a second since creation's awakening.

Yet in our heart's faith we know for a certainty
the precocious rains, like each and every
entity must renew, transform,
return eventually to the moment of destiny,
the ingenious ocean in the
ever-extending expanses of skies.

Reflection at Dawn

Rain . . . all my senses
apprehend the fiery
excitement of ageless trees
restive with the weight of green
sunrises on quivering leaves
the glistening flow
of silken water.

Though whispering
in voices seemingly
alien, i know for a certainty
they are conscious
as in the very core of my being
i too am deeply
sentient of unending
connections, unspeakable
fellowships.

Dawn Visitors

The tall trees awaken, emerging
from behind the curtain of mist,
still rubbing heavy eyes.

Drops of living water trickle
down veins of exultant leaves
shivering in a caressing breeze,

Squirrels emerge to squabble
over remnants
of last night's *cempedak.*

A pair of mynah cautiously
pick grains of rice from my open
palm; regular visitors.

Harmony

In the disparate world of noises, I seek
the incalculable silence of the eternal,

in the centre of engulfing darkness
the desperate glimmer of dawning light.

In the tragic turmoil of every
screaming, struggling soul I hear

unarticulated voices of pain and desire
grasping for intractable meaning.

Wherever I search in all directions
I realize not the harmonies of lost being.

To the core of my own miniscule self
In desperation I turn; its quiet rhythm

through each and every molecule sings
for me the chronicle of existence.

Mirza Ghalib's Lament

Across the dreamy distance I hear the muezzin,
remember his personal plea for me
to turn to Allah, praised be His Majesty.

The preacher reminds me each and every
pious day to direct my heart and unwilling
feet to his particular *masjid* and the remote
sacred *haram*, for in those directions,
it seems, lie the gateways to heaven, waiting
with its *houris*, even more tantalizing
than each and every courtesan of Hindustan
drunken rivers bounteous passing
leisurely through mesmerizing gardens.

Little do they realize that in my own
teeny voice I do talk to God Almighty;
in every verse sincerely sing praises
of His Creation. My one and only concern
is, whether or not as supreme poet Himself,
He condones my style of creativity.

Perchance one day I will meet Him face-
to-face without having first to die,
as maintain the *moulvis* and Sufis,
in a moment of ecstasy induced by a happy
balance between Delhi's best wine
and my appreciably complex utterances.

Perhaps then I will have an answer finally
from the Lord and Master directly
if indeed He is amenable to praises
of Himself and His fabulous Artistry, couched
in exceptional Persian or Urdu poetry.

Expectation

Today after unsounded decades
memories return, as if emerging
from some long forgotten dream;
shades of expectation, tall
as unassailable mountains, haunting
like unbridled Chinese phantoms.

The heart aches, apprehending
ruination that will not be touched
or felt or made sensible
in any way, but is there all the same
like some shadow falling
upon invisible expanses of time.

They come as reminder of what may
have been, what has become
along the long journey
from the beginning of desires,
the heart and soul confused
the sun, moon and stars silent as ever.

Precious Moments

Let us return to those precious moments
when the world was still young
the tablet of memory unstained

when the shining mirror of the heart
reflected creation's glory
unconstrained
we heard the music
of the spheres, drank
the giving fountain of youth

let us seize for ever those moments
of innocence; in those lies our wisdom,
on them depends our reason.

Restless at 4:05 a.m.

A strange restlessness stirs me
out of the empty silence of a night
in cautious reverie
to a world still slumbering.

I wonder what their dreams
are made of, what nightmares
they encounter; wonder
if they grasp the reality
that sleep and death are merely
twins, their visions possibly
more real than they will ever know.

I wonder if they will be any better
prepared to rise yet again to a
sumptuous serving of the ordinary
everyday mirage of reality.

Resonance

When in moments of sheer melancholy
I reflect upon my own being,
I realise I am nothing
but the resonance
of the song of destiny
sung in primordiality,
the burning desire of nonbeing
to express itself in some possibly
meaningful way.

Song of Existence

The glorious sun sings
its song of existence
it is the creator
it is the creation
it is the light that rejoicing
shines in the interior
labyrinths of the heart.

Moments

The moments pass glittering
like the light
of the silently whispering
moon upon gentle waters
chasing its own image
signaling something
I have neither
understood nor ever
will: the great mystery of time.

Quatrains

I

In these quiet moments heavy with yesteryear memories
your youthful presence visits, fresh as ever after endless days
and nights of separation, as if some breeze from heaven's garden
having lost its way, has flown into my soul's lonesome alleys.

II

The restless ocean, remembering suddenly the strain
of some ancient melody springs to life with a new urge, its voice
sounding the strings of my being in an urgency suggesting
all that is revived will soon be restored to silence once again.

III

This night of countless desires is like none other, wild urges
overwhelm the senses, crowd the streams of existence;
and when, at the crack of dawn, the seemingly endless
inebriation departs, what will become of restless passions?

IV

The day finds its way into the dark bosom of night
voices of the hours recede into realms of silence
only memories remain constant, fresh as essence
of rose, immortal, resisting inviolate canons of mutability.

V

This is my wish that having bid farewell I may return
time and again to your face in the mirror of my heart
evoking its first reflection there, before the ravages
of time cloud it with rust, weaken the light in my eyes.

Voiceless Night

Voiceless
night sits heavy and restless,
engulfing all existence,
the stars its countless
eyes watching,
like destiny itself.

Letter from the Past

A crispy clean epistle emerges
from the recesses,
a face from behind a veil
of memories. The greetings
are the same as ever, their voice
fresh as the first encounter
but the tone is different
somehow, no longer suggesting
freshness of dawn breezes
the perfume in the blushing paper
mellowed by long silence,
the passage of undetermined time.

Reality

Reality lies before us, smiling, familiar
as ever, a regular partner or lover.
We think we know each other;
a closer look unfolds
the fuzziness at the edges, the chasm
between one thing and another.

The known and unknown blur
into a synthesis, images out of focus
It is inevitable we begin all over,
travel the same path, wade through
accrued confusion in consciousness,
arrive at the same position.

Presence

The quietly breathing
hills listen intently to persistent
streams slithering hurriedly
down their verdant bodies
following last night's darkly
ferocious downpour.

A heavy presence lives
in the shadowy
expectation, unfamiliar
but nonetheless anticipated,
harbinger
of something portentous.

Meaning

The distances stretch away beyond the stars
beyond imagination, storing in their
darknesses and living lights the mysteries
of being beyond the mind's understanding.

Among them I belong, in them is inscribed
my name, written all that pertains to me
in the book of existence,
its pages seen solely by the eyes of destiny.

Beyond immensities of seeming emptinesses
crossing the furthest boundaries
the secret lights of the last stars dead and living
I yearn to pass, long to realize my meaning.

Message from a Leaf

Squatting uncomfortably
by the breezy lakeside, getting
to know the waters I have seen for ever
a leaf floats towards me.
I hear its barely
perceptible words: brother,
you and I are closer than you know
or ever will; I a yellowing leaf,
you lesser nor greater.

Your heartfelt poetry,
my unheralded whisper
come from the very same source,
the word that fashioned your being
gave rise to me. Farewell dear brother
until we meet again in another
time, another dimension.

Trembling, I pick up the leaf
in uncertain hand, fondle it, a wingless
bird; I embrace it close
to my heart and then set it free
in the water, let it go on its journey;
while I too move on, on my own.

Portrait

Your face alone glows
soft in the surrounding
darkness, the rest of you
dimmed, as if the departing
sun had left behind
some precious
ray of itself to brighten
my inner being
night after endless night

Night's Secrets

Following long communion
the night has gone,
making quiet way
for the hurrying dawn.
I sense her presence still,
remember
the secrets shared
between mutual companions,
in nuanced whispers
unknown to others.

These must remain darkly
hidden, learned
by the night at source
at time's very beginning.
These in confidence she
conveyed to me, directly;
for others there were
dewdrops nightly
shed, glittering tears
emblazoning her cheek.

Mystery

Half-hidden
behind the thin clouds
the moon
is a mysterious
damsel in a flimsy veil.
I wonder what she looks like,
wonder if I should write
a ghazal in her praise.

No. perhaps I should wait
in patience
for the morning breeze
to reveal her face.

Thunderstorm

It has been raining all evening
the sky sending
down in exuberance
its tears of joy or sadness,
one can never be certain.
But in my inner being
there is a sense of exultance
as every drop of sacred rain
attunes with its very own
melancholy strain
the familiar vibrations within.

The earth, jubilant
in its soaking greenness
after a parching day's pain,
slumbers wrapped in
silent coolness,
while the moon, peeping
through curtains of endless sky,
in silken tenderness
spreads over existence
calm and quiet following
the storm's intensity,
a blanket of drowsiness.

Book of Existence

I read a brand new book last evening
perhaps the hundredth this year
twenty thousandth since the written
word took possession of me, reading
became second nature,
I remember shifting from one
to another, or returning every
now and then to the same volume
the identical page or line even.

But I discovered over and over
again, beyond persistent voices
of words so soft and soothing
or strained to the extreme
I discerned nothing new in all
that has ever been read or written,
for everything worthy of knowing
it seems has always been there in essence
in the book of existence.

Question

See, I have come
before you again and again
in sunshine
or in pouring rain
but to seek an answer
to a question that remains
inconvenient, troublesome
and has always been so,
a question only
you can answer, unfolding
for me the mystery
of my being.

Boredom

In moments of unimaginable tedium
when not knowing what to do even
with my very own self I turn
in desperation, questioning,
to my interior beings, my other vaguely
known but yet unfamiliar identities.

And then I am never certain whether
I am the questioner or the questioned
the petitioner or the petitioned.
I am not even confident my persistent
questions are at all sensible,

if any answers will be forthcoming,
or if, on the contrary even the very
act of asking will not itself suddenly
become a risky uncontrollable thing,
a whirling worm in the mind.

But then what option is there
but to ask even if things
seem to be leading nowhere,
if only to gain a momentary sense
of fleeting lightness from the madness
of an insufferable moment.

Early Morning

The drowsy morning
like a troubled conscience
makes the day's
demands yet again
the alarm clock
passionately sounds
the repeated warning.

In the semidarkness
body and soul
both still half-asleep
or dreaming
contend with each other
for the last precious
dose of obliviousness.

Seasons

I long for changing seasons
with their returning cycles, options
to be fashionable, dress differently
like the earth herself
in her never-ending livery.

I seek multiplicities
of ambiance, their potentialities
to bestow diverse ways of being,
give rise to subtler senses,
enliven latent feelings.

But beyond yearning there is certainty
keener imagination, expanding
vision will reveal novel
varieties of poetry unrestrained
by limits to expressibility.

Garden

Tiny dewdrops
falling on my head
sink deep
into my interior
the stream of water
merging
in joyous encounter
of self-discovery
in the garden
of everlasting
mystery.

Hamlet

We have come across you
on the boards of many a theatre,
encountered you in the passionate heart
and spirit of every individual.
Yet you stand aloof beyond
common understanding,
Aristotelian theories, penetrating
Freudian analysis or mighty
intellectual capacities of many
a returning renaissance.

While extremely familiar to us,
Hamlet, you remain still an enigma,
caught between the dilemma
of two irreconcilable worlds,
no, not just two but too many
to tell, with the capacity
to break through your sensitive artistry,
your humanity, near-divinity.

While at an immense distance from us
you are simultaneously
too close to be seen or satisfactorily
fathomed. Yet, perhaps at some
moment when finally we recognize our own
true nature in the mirror of existence
we may see into the baffling
obscurity of your uneasy being.

Old Acquaintance

After the long-distance telephone call
as if out of nowhere, the strangely
anticipated meeting
turned out to be nothing at all
following enthusiastic expressions
of customary surprise.

Clear signs evidenced that time
had relentlessly reclaimed
what it had momentarily lent:
the body lean and bent,
the hair seriously thinning, the skin deeply
wrinkled, the smiles once scintillating,
toothless. One could not but yet again be
awed at nature's immense
capacities to marvelously create,
mercilessly decimate.

And if, leaving aside appearances
one had the faintest expectation things
would somehow be different
in the limitless interior with the ripening
in time, no matter how tardy,
of a tiny seed of wisdom,
here too awaited nothing
save disenchantment: the ability
at expression stymied, the memory
lapsing, the cavernous mind empty.

Nothing, it appeared, had remained
steady or altered for the better,
the ferocious energies, rather,
long set upon the path of fateful decline
would soon take everything
with them beyond the point of return.

Essentiality

Each and every flower abloom
in the dewy freshness
of a still-drowsy
dawn, each leaf falling
in the reflective silence
of a mellowing sunset, every
subtle note of a birdsong
in the fading distance
brings a reminder
from another garden,
one we see
nor sense in its essentiality.

Time

We speak of time as if it had
a beginning, of its ending at any
moment sooner or later, take seriously
now one, now another of many
a prediction or prophecy.

But these are notions surely
of petty souls, paltry minds,
fears and anxieties
of self expressed merely
to convince itself.

For it stands for a certainty
that time designed itself so very
judiciously, unlike any of its
creations, by no means ever to see
its own expiration in ignominy.

Sadness

I have scarcely
left you
when you come with me
sadness
from the root of the tree
of life rising in me
like the sap,
engulfing me,
until it appears
the two of us
will remain
inseparable companions
forever and ever.

Shadows

Shadows stretch endless
into drowsy
distances:
those of humanity,
mountains, trees
and all other symbols
or manifestations
of creation
all indistinguishable,
merging
into the one bold darkness
as the evening
assumes its mantle
of pure obscurity.

Dreams

Echoes of the day's voices
resonate in my interior, images
of all ages between
preexistence and existence
flow in a never-ending gallery
of master artworks in full lucidity
crossing frontiers, breaking
boundaries of time and space
as though I am present there
watching an exciting
theatre performance or a film
featuring known actors
confronting totally strange figures
out of the world's fabulous
literatures. Yet upon awakening
neither a shadow remains
nor even the faintest memory
of an extraordinary
nocturnal journey.

Departure

When the light leaves with
night's darkness engulfing
the living stars and every
earthly thing in its enduring
mantle, the mind turns
to the instant when it all
began, the enthralling
resonance of the first syllable,
the primal burst of brightness.

The ceasing of breath, shutting
of eyes, the glance turned
inward must surely
signify a return merely
to the very beginning,
the commencement of another
cycle in the moment
eternal, another movement
in the whirling dance of atoms.

Colours

A stirring array of hues
uncountable, mysterious
paints the living canvases
of earth and sky
each seeking
to outshine the others
even the shades of inner
universes, mirrors
of heart and mind.

Loneliness

Loneliness spreads
from out of vast unknown
deserts of emptiness
like the tiniest of dewdrops
finding their way
from endless skies
into secret hearts of flowers
melting into invisibility
yet overwhelming every
cell of body, every
unrealized drop of spirit.

Arrival and Departure

Every arrival
is a departure,
every fresh dawn,
each sinking evening
built by the pageant
of prancing moments
unrecognized,
imperceptible
until the prompting
of the last bell.

Thunderclap

The first thunderclap
of the still-dark
silently awakening
dawn
sings a song
of potential rain
the cleansing
of the world
a refreshing
expansion of spirit.

Beauty

I recall time and time again beauty
that once was there
and the light scent of smiling perfume
that regaling at once all senses, giving
liberation to the inner spirit of being
and gladness, beauty
that filled my very existence
to the brim, a sign of divinity
everywhere to be seen yet elusive
in its many shy manifestations.

Its going troubled me for countless
days beyond the moment
until a visionary notion that beauty
had furtively hidden solely
because I had failed to perceive
it in all its subtle hues
unending like changing
nuances of existence, coldly
attuned to what my senses sought
rather than wisdom revealed.

Connection

Each leaf falling
in the mellowing silence
of a meditative evening
is an enticement into realms
with which we
have possessed
a more than passing
acquaintance.

Memories

Memories flow in
with the swish of the whispering
tide, and when the ocean
leaves they remain
in excited sands, each grain
sensing a song fresh as ever,
each awaiting anxious
the arrival of the next ocean.
Thus remembrance of precious
being from one moment
to another gets written
in the book of eternity.

Song

Softly in the still awakening
dawn a song begins somewhere
unknown, a melody familiar
yet intractable, first heard aeons ago
in the voice of an unseen singer.

The song of the morning enters
into every cell of my being,
its subtle centre and beyond,
its vibrations reaffirming
connections with all that sings.

Violin

It is one of those unbearable
nights. The darkness
weighs down deeply
its subtle heaviness
greater even than the credence
of living. In all of this
ominous silence the only
sign of life, the melancholy
voice of an enticing violin,
reaches me from within
my inner being
or from some dimension
of unrealized existence.

Confused

I am not discontented with you
life, merely confused over
your imprecise signs, your
gestures so very innocent,
so appealing, yet possessing
power to harshly
change all so richly
cherished, like the newborn
smile of an infant turning
all at once for no seeming
reason into a stream of tears
issuing from restless seas
in the heart's mysterious valleys.

Inseparable

You and I sitting
in this evening
garden where the flowers
laugh and the birds sing
we feel the waters
flowing in the streams
as well as in life,
the waters of life singing
with us in one voice
with the creation.

Call of the Waters

I hear the waters call again
and again, the waters in the heavens,
the countless rivers and seas
the waters in the oceans
within me, calling
as they have been since
the miraculous moment of creation.
I see them dance, hear them sing
their song unaltered, sense
their longings to fuse once again
into the very first, the original drop.

Finality

The day draws to a close as usual
like each previous one completing
itself in a lively splash of embers;
but this evening
there is a vast difference
in the reflective, particularly
sober sky and its quietly alarming
colours as apprehensively
I watch the day leave, for this
seems to be the solemn finality
of something inexplicably
enormous, the irreversible setting
of an oft-lived yet vague dream.

Glossary

Bhava (Sanskrit)   Emotion

Cempedak (Malay)   Jackfruit

Ghazal (Arabic/Persian/Urdu)   A form of lyrical poetry

Masjid (Arabic)   Mosque, Muslim Prayer house

Haram (Arabic)   Sacred –esp with reference to the area around the Kaaba in Mecca

Houri (Persian)   Nymph

Moulvi (Urdu)   A preacher

PROF. DR. GHULAM-SARWAR YOUSOF

Personal Information

Prof. Dato' Dr. Ghulam-Sarwar Yousof graduated in English from the University of Malaya (1964), and did a Doctorate in Asian Theatre at the University of Hawaii (1976). He is one of Malaysia's most distinguished scholars of performing arts and one of the world's leading specialists of traditional Southeast Asian theatre.

He was responsible for setting up Malaysia's first Performing Arts programme at the Science University of Malaysia (USM) in Penang in 1970. Dato' Ghulam Sarwar Yousof served at that university as lecturer and Associate Professor. He joined the Cultural Centre, University of Malaya (UM) as Professor in 2002.

Currently, he is an Adjunct Professor at the Cultural Centre, University of Malaya, Kuala Lumpur. He is also Director of The Asian Cultural Heritage Centre Berhad, a private research initiative set up by him to promote research in traditional Asian cultures.

Apart from traditional Asian theatre, his major interests include Asian literatures, folklore studies, as well as South- and Southeast Asian cultures, comparative religion, mythology and, Sufism. In ethnographic and folklore studies he has explored Malay-Indonesian mythology and folk literature, Malay concepts of the soul (*semangat*), and *angin* as well as their place in healing processes involving traditional theatre.

As a creative writer, he has published poetry, drama as well as short stories. He has also done a translation of Kalidasa's Sanskrit play *Shakuntala* as well as translations of Urdu poetry into English. Among other things, he is currently working on a volume of ghazal translations into English as well as an anthology of Islamic Literature.

Dato' Ghulam-Sarwar Yousof's most outstanding contribution to academia is in traditional Southeast Asian Theatre. In this area he has carved a unique niche for himself, with meticulous field work and research in some previously unexplored genres, resulting in the most important existing publication on the subject, his *Dictionary of Traditional Southeast Asian Theatre* (Oxford 1994). His vast collection of fieldwork materials and documentation is currently held by the Asian Cultural Heritage Centre Berhad.

Dato' Ghulam-Sarwar Yousof has held visiting positions as professor at several universities, has lectured in many countries in both Asia and Europe on a broad spectrum of culture-related subjects and on altogether unclassifiable disciplines alike to absolute novices and specialized audiences. He has also given readings of his poetry and short stories as well as organized major poetry events in Kuala Lumpur and Penang in conjunction with UNESCO World Poetry Day. He has been, over the decades, involved in various capacities in numerous cultural organizations, national and international, including the Asia-Europe Foundation as Malaysia's official representative and member of the foundation's Board of Governors.

LITERARY PUBLICATIONS

1. Ghulam-Sarwar Yousof. *Perfumed Memories.* Singapore: Graham Brash Pte Ltd., 1982. (Collection of Poems)
2. Ghulam-Sarwar Yousof. *Halfway Road, Penang. Penang.* Teks Publishing Company, (1982). Reprinted by The Asian Cultural Heritage Centre, Penang, 2002. (Drama text).
3. Ghulam-Sarwar Yousof. *Mirror of a Hundred Hues: A Miscellany.* Penang: The Asian Cultural Heritage Centre, 2001.

4. Ghulam-Sarwar Yousof. *Songs for Shooting Stars: Mystical Verse.* Pittsburgh, PA 15222, USA: Lauriat Press, 2011. (Selected Poems).

5. Ghulam-Sarwar Yousof. *Transient Moments.* Kuala Lumpur: The Asian Cultural Heritage Centre, 2012. (Selected Poems)

6. Ghulam-Sarwar Yousof. (Editor). *The Asian Centre Anthology of Malaysian Poetry in English.* Singapore: Partridge, 2014.

7. Ghulam-Sarwar Yousof. *The Trial of Hang Tuah the Great: A Play in Nine Scenes.* Singapore" Partridge, 2014.

8. Ghulam-Sarwar Yousof. *Tok Dalang and Stories of Other Malaysians.* Singapore: Partridge, 2014.

9. Ghulam-Sarwar Yousof. *Suvarna-Padma.* Singapore: Partridge, 2015

Poems in Anthologies

Dato' Ghulam-Sarwar Yousof's poems have also been included in the following anthologies:

- Thumboo, Edwin (ed). *The Second Tongue: An Anthology of Poetry from Malaysia and Singapore.* Singapore: Heinemann, 1976.
- Hashmi, Alamgir (ed). *The Worlds of Muslim Imagination.* Islamabad: Gulmohar, 1986.
- Malachi, Edwin (ed). *Insight: Malaysian Poems.* Petaling Jaya: Maya Press, 2003.

- Maya Press. *The Spirit of the Keris.* Petaling Jaya: Maya Press, 2003.
- Rosli Talif and Noritah Omar (ed). *Petals of Hibiscus: A Representative Anthology of Malaysian Literature in English.* Petaling Jaya: Pearsons Malaysia Sdn Bhd, 2003.
- Thumboo, Edwin (ed). *& Words: Poems Singapore and Beyond.* Singapore: Ethos Books, 2010.
- Ghulam-Sarwar Yousof (ed). *The Asian Centre Anthology of Malaysian Poetry in English.* Singapore: Partridge, 2014.

Random Poems Published

Random poems have appeared in the following journals:

- *Lidra* (Kuala Lumpur)
- *Mele* (Honolulu)
- *Impulse* (Honolulu)
- *Pacific Quarterly* (Hamilton, New Zealand)
- *Dewan Sastera* (Kuala Lumpur)
- *Solidarity* (Manila)

Short Stories

"Lottery Ticket", "Birthday", "Tok Dalang" and "Dewi Ratnasari" in **Mirror of a Hundred Hues: A Miscellany.** Penang: The Asian Centre, 2001.

Printed in the United States
By Bookmasters